LOST LETTERS IN MAIL

A COLLECTION OF TRAGEDIES

MAITREYEE RIYA

To everyone who did not have the courage to show their artistic
side to others,

Contents

Acknowledgements

I'd like to acknowledge all the writers whose books i grew up reading.

Thank you, mum and dad, well for everything;

My not-so-beloved sister for spreading positivity around me, always trying to be the better version of yourself and inspiring others around you to do the same;

My niece, Aadya Mishra aka Jerry for being the sweetest person ever and listening to my rants all the time, not so much for being taller than me though

My friend, Snehil Jha, for being annoyingly optimistic.

Thank you, Shreshtha Ranjan, for encouraging me to do this.

Thank you, Shashwat Rajan, for being a constant. If i differentiate you, you'll become zero, which you are. Hahaha lol.

This is too cliche for me and I hope I don't have to write something like this ever again. But, here it is.

Prologue

A COLLECTION OF TRAGEDIES

Each poem has a story to tell. This book is like stepping onto a roller coaster; hesitant at first but it'll be a ride to remember. Throughout its journey, nostalgic memories circling round and round your head will make you dizzier than the ride itself.

You will feel a rush of emotions, making you recall your experiences; buried deep down in your subconscious.

Slowly but steadily, you'll find yourself completely immersed in the poems and form a special connection to each one of them.

1. CAMOUFLAGE

This place seems
Unfamiliar and strange now.
Or, is it you?
I wished to be here,
wished to be with you,
every day in these past two years.
It's scary.
For all, I can recall
are these small houses
with bricked walls,
wild plants climbing up the walls,
beside the railway tracks
and, acres of grasslands.
A perfect home for someone waiting
for their loved ones,
like the wife of an army officer,
waiting for his arrival,
soon after every war ends.
And, there is peace
in exchange for bloodshed
and deathbed,
hoping she doesn't have to,
after a very long wait,

open the door,
decorated with longing,
hours of sitting;
often getting lost
in a mere mirage of him,
to a dead body
Or any other bad news,
wrapped in red of
Olive green, brown.
The white flowers
on his deathbed
and, multiple gunshot wound on his chest,
singing triumphs of his bravery.
Those houses
have an '**abandoned**' sign
in bold, black letters
which makes me question
everything beautiful there is.
Does it always come with a
Everything broken Starter pack?

2. TRAFFIC LOVE LIGHT

365 days,

a flashback

in one heartbeat.

Thoughts running crazy,

roundabout in circles.

Taking a moment, sometimes.

Blinking headlights

and cars racing at high speed

like a roller coaster

cut loose,

a carousel,

I could see the

wrong turns clearly,

with my eyes wide open.

The red lights

giving me a warning

to stop.

But, you and I

drunk in love,

color-blind,

ignoring all the signs,

chasing towards a home,

our wrong love could cave in.
Sitting in driver's seat
without seatbelts on,
not knowing where
the brakes were.
Likely to crash,
our love was a train wreck
and so were we.
I could see
the yellow lights
from a distance,
telling us to slow down
but did we?
I guess not.
As we moved
the outside a blur,
a mix of colors
like an abstract painting
telling me stories
of all wrong loves',
left incomplete.
but we were ready to
take our love to crazy town
back and forth
and make it through
alive, unshattered
weren't we?

The car crashed.
We were thrown out
of our driver's seats,
up above in the air,
till we hit the ground.
Bruises all over our body.
Us,
exchanging glances,
breaking out in laughter,
craziness,
as you may call it
but, love is crazy.
Isn't it?
Our wrong love didn't know any boundaries.
The traffic lights didn't have
any power over us.
Something about it,
the rush,
the high,
that we would kill
to be crazy
in and out of love,
in mere memory.
Smiling at one another,
we saw the green light
knowing,
we beat our odds

and were good to go.
Our wrong love
found a way
through all the
right places.
Till another car crash.

3. LOST AGES REUNITE HERE

I saw you at the bookshop,
the one I went to,
wandering the streets of Paris
until my eye caught
the handcrafted
'lost ages reunites here' board
written in French.
Pink dahlias climbing up the walls.
The bookstore, my heart.
The vintage setting
with wooden hardwood flooring
red lights flickering,
hanging from the ceiling,
classical music playing
taking you back to the 1820s.
A composition by
Ludwig van Beethoven,
the kind of music
unraveling into your soul
so deeply,
you can hear the waves rising,
birds, chirruping

and your heart beating.
The smell of the coffee brewing
from across the street,
filling the bookstore
with a pleasant aura.

I was looking through
the stack piles of books
in the classic section,
stuck between two shelves,
a safe place.
I was flipping through the pages
when I saw you, Rose.
on the other side of the shelf,
sitting in the corner,
on a tiny wooden table,
gazing at the book.
The strands of your hair
falling onto it
your coffee getting cold,
But you, too busy to notice
Should I say something?
I dare not.
You had a flower bracelet
wrapped around your wrist
carrying a breathtaking scent

A lot like the

collection of love letters

in my hand,

sky blue ribbon

on its cover.

your beautiful white dress,

highlighting your collarbone.

you looked so pretty

van Gogh and Monnet

would fly across countries

to paint a beautiful canvas,

in the name of you.

the kind of portraits,

those small rooms in museums

are full of.

You were smiling

through the pages

in between the punctuations.

I watched the clock ticking

as the hours passed,

loving every second of it.

The poetry reading was about to start.

You just finished your book.

The audience settled into the small cubicle

of a large cafe with soft acoustics,

dim lights, and a little champagne
to lead you through the night.
Two strangers each
at one table.
There's a strange sense of high and magic in all of it.
You know what they do, Rose?
Who?
The poets.
They imagine a whole universe
full of alternate endings
where heartbreaks are beautiful
and love does make sense.
Don't you wonder?
Who is it, the source of their muse?
I do,
and it keeps me up at night,
making a funny face.
We laughed hysterically at the sheer thought of it.

Last time I kissed you
you smelled like coffee and cigarettes
with a hint of whipped cream
you had in the morning
your lips tasted like longing
weaved into a goodbye.
caffeine in your eyes,

and the smirk in your laughter
while you talk about dead poets
and old-school romance
made that midnight in Paris
worth it,
just for a little while.
you just had a bottle of whiskey
we bought from the store
on the 17th Victoria Street
The alcohol in your system
hid everything you were feeling,
The red in your eyes couldn't.
much like the ink
from 'Romeo and Juliet' recreated.

I hope I don't meet you again
For I wanna keep this
beautiful image of you
in my memory, untouched.

4. DISTANT

The memory of the
last day i met you ,
Still fresh like
the wind after rain,
cold and shievering,
yet romantic.
It was 3rd of July.
I snuck out of my house
to meet you,
one last time.
We were walking
down the streets in silence
with a weird, nauseous
feeling in our chest.
Our minds, full of thoughts
and millions of questions
bothering us
like the mosquito at night
buzzing through the space
Yet, we were speechless.
The traffic lights
and honking cars,
The rush on the crossing

were the only sound that could be heard.
Our eyes traced the little shops
on either sides of the road,
the people on the footpath,
the lady with the hat,
nor once,
did they meet.
Why?
Maybe because we were afraid
of the emotions that would make its way through
a moment of weakness.
22 minutes passed.
We reached a cafe,
climbed up the stairs
and made our way
through the front door.
It was a room full of people.
Some of them discussing business proposals,
a couple arguing over how much they
hated this place.
So did we, i guess.
There was an empty table
on the very far right corner.
We sat there,
You were playing with my hair clip
the whole time.
I put my head on your chair

and tried to remember
that exact moment
as precisely as possible.
A photographic memory,
if i must say so.
Telling my heart to take note.
It was time for me to go
I thought of many ways
we could have said goodbye.
But, we didn't.
We didn't make any
heavy duty promises.
Just that, we would give this a shot.
When i finally left,
the distance between us
getting bigger and bigger,
with every shop passing by.
It hit me,
the rush of emotions,
my heart pounding heavily,
veins about to explode,
all at once.
It is said that when you die,
you start recalling the
important moments in your memory.
That was one of those moments.
Every second with you

started playing in my head,
like a videotape, a camera film.
I looked back
and you,
slowily but steadily,
faded away.
And ,the distance took over.

5. YELLOW, AN ODD COLOR

I sat in the cab,

The yellow one

with blinking red headlights.

Trees moving past me,

luggage sitting beside

and, your bracelet wrapped around my wrist.

Funny,

How this new town,

painted with raindrops,

pretty pink wild flowers

clear blue skies,

parks on each corner

Of the streets,

opening into another.

You never get lost here.

Anywhere you go,

It leads you back to

where you started.

Like a puzzle put together.

Each piece,

fitting perfectly,

Unlike us,

Making sense

One after another.

Everything beautiful

turned into a cozy little home.

When I first arrived

At this no rain city,

It was raining in that part of the city.

You see the irony

The kind of weather that

makes you want to

have some cheap wine

or a hot cup of coffee

with your lover.

Cabs dripping wet with raindrops

raincoats and umbrellas,

blue and yellow.

Roads filled with stack of water.

Thunder roaring loud.

Lightning strikes.

As I move to the other side

To wrap my arms around you.

But, you weren't there

An empty and hollow feeling.

much like the water bottle

In my hand.

Tears mixed with rain.

How much I hated boarding that train

With our last conversation,

Playing on my mind

Over and over again.

I could see the numbness in your eyes

And, your actions

as I stood there,

Clueless on the platform.

The arrival of the train was announced.

My heart started beating faster.

Delay or cancel the train ,maybe?

6. IN THE MEMORY OF YOU

Yesterday,
i was looking through
all of my stuffs,
reminiscing
old, forgotten memories.
Good old days,
as you may call it.
When i came across
a box sitting
with your name
engraved in it, Scarlett.
In golden letters.
In the corner of the closet,
left untouched,
over the years.
The box was decorated with
silver linings.
It has your scent,
your lavender rich perfume,
filling the space,
taking me back
to the night we met.

It was a quiet, lonely night.
You were screaming
out of the window
from the backseat of my car,
singing 'northern lights' by James young,
playing on the radio of the car.
Your hair driving you crazy
and you, me.
You were so full of life,
enjoying every moment
like it's the end of the world.
Truth being told,
I was jealous of you, scar
you could make each minute count,
magical
while I simply hadn't
figured out who I am.

I remember you smiling at me
from across the table
of the abandoned bar we went to
No crowd,
just like we liked it.
vodka and gin tonic

in the glass in front of us.
you ordered a round of tequilla
and spilled it
all over your favorite dress
oh, how you cried all the way home.
That dress is still safe with me
wrapped in a air tight sheet
away from all the dust.
I still have
the playlist you made for me
on a crushed colored sheet,
the love letters you wrote to me,
while you were away
on a business trip.
And
your favorite novel
covered with coffee stains
and, dead flower bookmarks,
in the bottom shelf of my drawer.
I read it again and again
to understand
what about it
made you an insomniac.
I never knew why.
I can see our love
sitting fragmented in pieces,
thinking where did that love go?

Nowhere, i guess.
It is still
locked away,
somewhere deep inside our hearts,
right where it belongs.
Life, for me was simple and dull
until i met you.
God, how could you make everything look so easy.
You were a wanderer and i, a loner.
Something about it
didn't quite entwine.
Our hands too.
We were two imperfect people
trying to make sense.
Your ocean blue eyes
sparkling in the
new York city lights.

7. SUMMERTIME ROMANCE

It's summer again
bright sunny day.
The sky outside was blue
shining on
and above us.
We were walking by the sidewalk,
stopping every now and then,
noticing the kids play
in the scorching heat.
Adults watching them,
with a half-smile on their face
giving us nostalgia,
reminding us of when we were kids.
My hair was tied into a bun,
loose ends hanging from the corners.
His light brown hair,
waving up and down
in a perfect wave.
Sweat covering our face
and his shirt.
Often, a sudden cold wind
approached us, giving us chills.

We stopped for a while
under a tree.
In front of us was a white house,
old little cottage,
giving us the retro vibe
orchids by the fences
one of our favorites
and a little garden
all the way
to the front door.
All the pretty flowers,
white and yellow,
dazzling in the sun.

We were sitting
on the cracked bench,
under the tree,
when i saw an ice cream cart
passing by,
and dragged you to it.
Filled with a plethora of joy,
doing that little dancing
while strolling through the streets,
a butter scotch cone
in my hand
and yours, a black currant.

I was wearing
a ripped blue denim
and a red off shoulder top
that day
and you, in a white shirt
and blue jeans.
Your sweet aroma
like a cup of hot morning latte,
warming the palms of my hand.
you turned your head towards me
and the sun lit up in your eyes.
Warm brown eyes.
Giving a sweet comfort,
much needed
to my heart.

Moments later,
we reached a turning
across the street.
Our houses
the other ways,
hugging goodbye
with a hesitation
that could be seen
all over our face,
into our eyes

and, the stammering
while we spoke
a few lines.
I could think of countless
metaphors of parting,
running in and out of my mind.
Thinking,
is this it?
We made no promises
too afraid
of keeping them
or failing
and, eventually drowning?
Set in different directions,
our paths separated.
I saw him changing lanes
after a few steps.
I looked back
but, he was too far gone
nowhere to be seen.
Disappearing
into the crowd.
As I look at it,
I can't help
but wonder,
Was he real or a mere mirage ?

One year later,
it's summer again.
I passed across
the same sidewalk,
watching those same kids
who grew in height,
a song playing on my mind
on repeat,
unable to recall the lyrics,
just the tune,
went on and on
in my head.
I stopped at the
same old white cottage.
I could see a to-let sign
hanging, swinging by in the air.
I made my way toward the door
and knocked.
I didn't know what I was doing
but, my conscience
told me not to stop.
I bought that house
with a warm feeling in my chest
and hope
that someday, he may come again.
He will know where to look for me.

And if he doesn't, that's okay.
But maybe,
someday.
Till then, I will keep on wondering,
Was this just my summer love?
or
Will he come to make this house
A home once again?

Every day,
I watered the lawns,
set the dining table
and,
sit for hours and hours,
on the wooden chair
that creaked,
watching every person passing by
in the hope
to see a familiar face,
soon
or
someday.
His face.
That hot summer day of June,
still imprinted in my memory,
like the fresh air

of 5 AM,

like a set of polaroids

you skim through

when you get old

and wrinkled.

'Summertime sadness' by Lana Del Ray

playing on the radio.

Every time there was a knock,

my heart fluttered,

to break

a few moments later.

When the sun set

and it was dark again,

with shimmering stars around,

till it's midnight

up until 2 AM sometimes.

I went to bed disappointed

getting very little

or no sleep.

That was my daily routine

A few years passed,

those kids don't play anymore

there is another set of kids

playing in the field.

The old man

who originally owned the house,

passed away.

Little by little,
the things around me
changed.
So did the people.
It was my birthday.
I was baking some
cookies and cakes,
and setting the dinner table,
when I heard a knock.
By now,
I had gotten used to being disappointed
anyway,
I approached towards
the door
and flew it open
And,
there he was.
standing with orchids in his hand,
wearing a white shirt
and blue jeans.
He said,
"I finally found you,
missed me much?"

8. CLICHE

You made infinite spelling errors
and I, a grammar nazi.
Timing is an art,
but, you and i,
not much of an artist,
you see.
It didn't make sense
but now,
It does.
only if I could,
I would
paint a canvas
flowing with bright colors
in the name of you
with brushes, thick and thin
and color pallets
filled with
vibrant shades of you.
The sprinkle of water
defining your purity.
You are the equation
so beautifully made,
I can't solve

but I'll trytill my last breath
and
whatever beyond.
My heart is a mess.
Mind, a maze.
And, you are the center of it.
You are like origami,
a simple colored sheet
at first,
turned into something beautiful,
with folds,
twists and turns,
adding glitters and sparkles
to my life.
A piece of artwork.

9. GALAXIES IN OUR EYES

As I lay here
completely blank,
empty-minded,
on my terrace floor,
under a sky
full of stars,
Crescent-shaped moon,
lots of known constellation,
a few unknown ones.
The Ursa Major and Orion,
the pheonix and centaur.
Some simple,
some complex.
And then there were others,
the zodiac sign ones,
Virgo and Sagittarius.
I read a thing or two
about constellations
in an astronomy book.
And I recalled
how I wanted to be an astronaut,
mesmerized by the beauty of

stars, galaxies
and, space beyond that.
Pulling in all-nighters
Just to look through the telescopes.
Making out as many constellations
as I could,
was supposedly my favorite
thing in the world.
Sometimes,
somedays,
when I used to have a bad day,
I would just go
and lie down on my terrace floor,
just watching the stars
aligning beautifully.
If lucky,
a shooting star maybe,
made my heart feel at ease.
In that moment,
I forgot
everyone
and
everything.
without a worry
without a doubt
I was happy.
But, the scare afterward,

Mortifying.
You feel like
you have nowhere else to go to
because all you have left is
a mind full of hurt, lies
and heartbreak.
Shattering dreams,
nightmares shaping themselves into reality,
monsters masked all around,
your evil self
exposing your dark side,
an empty feeling in your stomach
and
all the butterflies
flying away.
Heartache.
A sudden wave
of darkness, emptiness
hits you.
You find yourself in
a constant battle.
You and your intrusive thoughts.
Who will win?
I leave it for you to decide.

10. SEALED, SCENTED

These empty perfume bottles
sitting on the racks
Beautifully engraved name
some with cute little laced ribbons on top
the way they still smell the same
reminds me of
every happy memory
I had with you.
The black dress I wore to your funeral
which I bought for your anniversary
lies hanging in the cupboard
I matched those
with a pair of black dangling earrings
and black pumps
only you could understand
my die-hard love for black.
the golden locket you gave me
still has our black and white picture.
The last cigarette you smoked
is safe with me
along with your journal
filled with pages
chocolate wrappers and pressed flowers

in the box, you adored so much

And your mix tape

full of old melancholy

You'd play it on the radio and make me listen to it

anytime, anywhere

Be it midsummer rain

or the first snow,

or the chilly winters.

You'd start dancing around like crazy

like a wild animal cut loose,

dragging me with you,

all the time.

It was raining

the day of your funeral.

My coat, drenched with water

My hair, too.

I had to give this whole speech

My eyes, wet with tears

Nobody noticed I guess.

The rain was my savior.

Guess our love for rain did its magic.

I sat by your grave

for hours after everyone left.

Hey,

I brought orchids to your grave,

just like I promised.

I have locked my love for you

in an empty perfume bottle.
Your favorite one.
It's filled with scented memories.
I watched the sunset and the day end.
See you on the other side.

11. GRAVEYARD OF LOVE

When I enter your room,
It seems like a lost cause.
A graveyard of our love.
Your sweet scent filling the air.
You, not here to fill the void.
The empty space in the cupboard
and, the other side of the bed
calls for you,
like a ghost screaming out
for her lover.
The polaroids,
pictures of you and me,
where we loooked happy.
Two smiling faces,
pinned to the small notice board,
on the wall above the desk.
Quite colorful,
a lot like you.
Fairy lights around it glowing,
every time I switch off the lights.
As I am lying in this darkened room,
looking at the starry ceiling

Imagining you, lying beside me
our hands, almost touching,
talking about love and everything beautiful
under the stars.
Our eyes shining brighter.
Completely clueless
of the scary night
full of nightmares.
Ghost of you haunting me,
every step of the way.
Letters to you
lying on the desk,
like spilled water on the floor.
Slippery.
The bedsheets had those
Cute little smileys on them.
The ones you fought
With me over for.
Your green bottle
reflecting your face.
With water
half filled, half rotten.
It has been sitting beside the bed
for days now.
I didn't want to
throw it away.
For it would have been like

throwing something of you
and,
I've got only your belongings,
the memories in my head,
rhe conversations in the text,
to hold onto you,
to the love I have for you.
I am writing
all these poems,
Spilling ink like words
in my sleep.
Romanticizing our love.
The love I can't have.